ARTERIAL BLOOD GAS

TABLE OF CONTENTS

INTRODUCTION

Arterial blood gases (ABGs) are a crucial diagnostic tool in the realm of healthcare, offering valuable insights into a patient's respiratory and metabolic state. This book, "Mastering Arterial Blood Gases: A Comprehensive Guide for Healthcare Providers," aims to demystify the complexities surrounding ABGs, making them accessible and understandable for healthcare professionals at all levels. Whether you are a seasoned clinician or a student just beginning your journey in healthcare, this book is designed to provide you with the knowledge and skills needed to effectively interpret and utilize ABG results in clinical practice.

The significance of arterial blood gases cannot be overstated. They are essential in assessing the adequacy of ventilation, oxygenation, and acid-base balance in patients. ABGs can reveal a multitude of conditions, from respiratory disorders like chronic obstructive pulmonary disease (COPD) and asthma to metabolic disturbances such as diabetic ketoacidosis and renal failure. Understanding ABGs is not just about reading numbers; it's about connecting those numbers to the patient's clinical condition and making informed decisions to optimize patient care.

This book is structured to guide you through the fundamental concepts and advanced applications of ABGs. Each lesson is meticulously crafted to build upon the previous one, ensuring a comprehensive understanding of the subject matter. We begin with an introduction to the basics of arterial blood gases, including what they are and why they are important. From there, we delve into the physiology of blood gases, exploring how they are produced, transported, and regulated within the body.

MODULE ONE

LESSON ONE: ARTERIAL BLOOD GASES

Arterial blood gases (ABGs) are a cornerstone of clinical diagnostics, providing critical information about a patient's respiratory and metabolic status. This will introduce the fundamental concepts of ABGs, laying the groundwork for the more detailed discussions in subsequent lessons.

What are Arterial Blood Gases?

Arterial blood gases are a series of tests that measure the levels of oxygen (O_2), carbon dioxide (CO_2), and the acidity (pH) of arterial blood. These parameters are essential in assessing how well the lungs are able to move oxygen into the blood and remove carbon dioxide from the blood. The primary components of ABGs include:

- pH: Indicates the acidity or alkalinity of the blood.
- PaO_2: Partial pressure of oxygen, reflecting the amount of oxygen gas in the blood.
- $PaCO_2$: Partial pressure of carbon dioxide, indicating how well carbon dioxide is able to move out of the body.
- HCO_3^-: Bicarbonate, a form of carbon dioxide that helps maintain the pH balance in the blood.
- SaO_2: Oxygen saturation, showing the percentage of hemoglobin molecules in the blood that are saturated with oxygen.

Importance of ABGs

Understanding and interpreting ABGs is vital for diagnosing and managing a variety of conditions, including:

- Respiratory disorders: Conditions like COPD, asthma, and pulmonary embolism can significantly alter blood gas levels.

- Metabolic disorders: Diabetic ketoacidosis, renal failure, and other metabolic conditions affect the acid-base balance.
- Critical care: In intensive care settings, ABGs are frequently used to monitor the respiratory status of critically ill patients.

Historical Perspective

The development of arterial blood gas analysis has a rich history, rooted in the advances of respiratory physiology and clinical chemistry. The ability to measure blood gases accurately has evolved significantly over the past century, from rudimentary techniques to sophisticated automated analyzers.

The Basics of Blood Gas Production and Transport

Blood gases are produced as a result of cellular metabolism. Oxygen is taken up by the lungs during inhalation and transported by hemoglobin in the red blood cells to tissues throughout the body. Carbon dioxide, a byproduct of cellular respiration, is transported back to the lungs and expelled during exhalation.

The regulation of blood gases involves complex physiological mechanisms, including the buffering systems that maintain pH within a narrow range, the respiratory system that controls the levels of CO_2, and the renal system that regulates bicarbonate concentration.

Overview of ABG Analysis Procedure

The process of obtaining an ABG sample involves:

- Preparation: Explaining the procedure to the patient, ensuring they are comfortable and calm.
- Sampling: Using a sterile syringe and needle to draw arterial blood, typically from the radial artery.
- Handling: Transporting the sample quickly to minimize changes in gas levels.
- Analysis: Using a blood gas analyzer to measure the parameters of interest.

MODULE TWO

LESSON ONE: THE PHYSIOLOGY OF

BLOOD GASES

Understanding the physiology behind blood gases is crucial for interpreting ABG results accurately. This lesson will delve into the mechanisms of gas exchange, transport, and regulation within the body.

The Respiratory System

The primary function of the respiratory system is to facilitate gas exchange between the atmosphere and the bloodstream. This involves:

- Ventilation: The movement of air into and out of the lungs.
- Diffusion: The transfer of oxygen and carbon dioxide between the alveoli and the blood.
- Perfusion: The flow of blood through the pulmonary capillaries.

Alveolar Gas Exchange

Gas exchange occurs in the alveoli, tiny air sacs in the lungs where oxygen is absorbed into the blood, and carbon dioxide is released from the blood. This process is driven by the partial pressure gradients of the gases: oxygen moves from areas of higher concentration in the alveoli to lower concentration in the blood, while carbon dioxide moves in the opposite direction.

Oxygen Transport

Once oxygen enters the bloodstream, it is transported in two forms:

- Dissolved in plasma: A small fraction of oxygen is dissolved directly in the blood plasma.
- Bound to hemoglobin: The majority of oxygen binds to hemoglobin molecules within red blood cells. Each hemoglobin molecule can carry up to four oxygen molecules, forming oxyhemoglobin.

The oxygen-hemoglobin dissociation curve describes the relationship between the partial pressure of oxygen (PaO_2) and the saturation of hemoglobin (SaO_2). Factors such as pH, temperature, and levels of 2,3-bisphosphoglycerate (2,3-BPG) can shift this curve, affecting oxygen delivery to tissues.

Carbon Dioxide Transport

Carbon dioxide is transported from the tissues to the lungs in three main forms:

- Dissolved in plasma: About 10% of CO_2 is transported in this form.
- Carbaminohemoglobin: Approximately 20% of CO_2 binds to hemoglobin.
- Bicarbonate: The majority (about 70%) of CO_2 is converted to bicarbonate (HCO_3^-) in red blood cells by the enzyme carbonic anhydrase.

Acid-Base Balance

The body maintains a tight regulation of pH through buffering systems, respiratory compensation, and renal compensation:

- Buffering systems: The bicarbonate buffer system is the primary extracellular buffer, reacting with excess acids or bases to maintain pH.
- Respiratory compensation: Changes in respiratory rate and depth can alter CO_2 levels, affecting the acid-base balance. For example, hyperventilation decreases CO_2 (and H^+),

leading to respiratory alkalosis, while hypoventilation increases CO2, leading to respiratory acidosis.

- Renal compensation: The kidneys regulate the excretion of hydrogen ions and the reabsorption of bicarbonate, adjusting the blood's acid-base status over a longer period.

MODULE THREE

LESSON ONE: COMPONENTS OF ARTERIAL BLOOD GASES

In this lesson, we will explore the individual components of arterial blood gases (ABGs) in detail. Understanding each parameter and its clinical significance is crucial for accurate interpretation and effective patient management.

pH: The Measure of Acidity

The pH of blood is a measure of its acidity or alkalinity. It reflects the concentration of hydrogen ions (H+) in the blood. The normal range for arterial pH is 7.35 to 7.45. Values below 7.35 indicate acidosis, while values above 7.45 indicate alkalosis. The body tightly regulates pH through buffer systems, respiratory adjustments, and renal compensation.

- Acidosis: Can result from respiratory causes (e.g., hypoventilation) or metabolic causes (e.g., lactic acidosis, diabetic ketoacidosis).
- Alkalosis: Can result from respiratory causes (e.g., hyperventilation) or metabolic causes (e.g., vomiting, diuretic use).

PaO2: Partial Pressure of Oxygen

The partial pressure of oxygen (PaO2) measures the amount of oxygen gas in arterial blood. The normal range is 75 to 100 mmHg. PaO2 provides insight into how well oxygen is being transferred from the lungs to the blood.

- Hypoxemia: Low PaO2 levels indicate hypoxemia, which can result from respiratory disorders like pneumonia, pulmonary embolism, or chronic obstructive pulmonary disease (COPD).
- Hyperoxia: High PaO2 levels, often due to excessive oxygen supplementation, can be harmful, especially in neonates and patients with chronic respiratory conditions.

PaCO2: Partial Pressure of Carbon Dioxide

The partial pressure of carbon dioxide (PaCO2) measures the amount of carbon dioxide gas in arterial blood. The normal range is 35 to 45 mmHg. PaCO2 reflects the effectiveness of ventilation.

- Hypercapnia: Elevated PaCO2 levels indicate hypoventilation and can lead to respiratory acidosis. Causes include obstructive lung diseases, central nervous system depression, and neuromuscular disorders.
- Hypocapnia: Low PaCO2 levels indicate hyperventilation and can lead to respiratory alkalosis. Causes include anxiety, pain, and central nervous system lesions.

HCO3-: Bicarbonate

Bicarbonate (HCO3-) is a key component of the blood's buffering system, helping to maintain pH balance. The normal range is 22 to 26 mEq/L. Bicarbonate levels indicate the metabolic component of acid-base balance.

- Metabolic Acidosis: Decreased HCO3- levels can result from conditions like diabetic ketoacidosis, renal failure, and severe diarrhea.
- Metabolic Alkalosis: Increased HCO3- levels can result from vomiting, diuretic use, and excessive bicarbonate administration.

SaO2: Oxygen Saturation

Oxygen saturation (SaO2) measures the percentage of hemoglobin molecules in the blood that are saturated with oxygen. The normal range is 95% to 100%. SaO2 provides a snapshot of how well oxygen is being carried to tissues.

- Desaturation: SaO2 levels below 90% indicate hypoxemia, which can be caused by respiratory or cardiac conditions, or low ambient oxygen levels.

Base Excess (BE) and Base Deficit (BD)

Base excess (BE) and base deficit (BD) are calculated values that reflect the metabolic component of acid-base balance. They indicate the amount of excess or deficit in the buffering capacity of the blood.

- Base Excess: Positive BE values indicate metabolic alkalosis or compensation for respiratory acidosis.
- Base Deficit: Negative BD values indicate metabolic acidosis or compensation for respiratory alkalosis.

Anion Gap

The anion gap is a calculated value that helps identify the cause of metabolic acidosis. It is calculated using the formula:

The normal range is 8 to 12 mEq/L. An elevated anion gap suggests the presence of unmeasured anions, often seen in conditions like lactic acidosis, ketoacidosis, and toxin ingestion.

Clinical Applications and Interpretation

Interpreting ABG results involves integrating information from all these components to understand the patient's overall respiratory and metabolic status. A systematic approach to ABG interpretation includes:

- Assessing pH: Determine if the patient is acidotic or alkalotic.
- Evaluating PaCO2 and HCO3-: Identify whether the primary disturbance is respiratory or metabolic.
- Checking for Compensation: Determine if the body is compensating for the primary disturbance.

- Calculating the Anion Gap: If metabolic acidosis is present, calculate the anion gap to narrow down the potential causes.

MODULE FOUR

LESSON ONE: INDICATIONS FOR ARTERIAL BLOOD GAS ANALYSIS

Arterial blood gas (ABG) analysis is a vital diagnostic tool used across various clinical settings. Understanding when and why to perform an ABG test is crucial for healthcare providers, as it helps in diagnosing and managing numerous conditions. This lesson will explore the indications for ABG analysis, detailing specific clinical scenarios where ABGs provide essential insights.

Respiratory Conditions

ABG analysis is commonly indicated in the assessment and management of respiratory disorders. It provides critical information about ventilation, oxygenation, and acid-base balance.

Chronic Obstructive Pulmonary Disease (COPD)

Patients with COPD often experience chronic respiratory insufficiency. ABG analysis helps in:

- Assessing the severity of hypoxemia and hypercapnia.
- Monitoring the effectiveness of oxygen therapy and ventilation support.
- Detecting acute exacerbations and guiding their management.

Asthma

In acute asthma exacerbations, ABG analysis is used to:

- Evaluate the degree of airway obstruction.
- Detect hypoxemia and hypercapnia, which indicate severe exacerbations.

- Guide the escalation of therapy, including the need for mechanical ventilation.

Acute Respiratory Distress Syndrome (ARDS)

ARDS is a severe lung condition characterized by diffuse alveolar damage and hypoxemia. ABG analysis is essential for:

- Assessing the severity of hypoxemia.
- Guiding the adjustment of ventilator settings.
- Monitoring the response to therapeutic interventions, such as prone positioning and high-frequency ventilation.

Metabolic Conditions

ABG analysis is also crucial in diagnosing and managing metabolic disorders, particularly those affecting acid-base balance.

Diabetic Ketoacidosis (DKA)

In patients with DKA, ABG analysis helps in:

- Confirming metabolic acidosis and determining its severity.
- Monitoring the response to insulin therapy and fluid resuscitation.
- Detecting complications such as hypokalemia and hyperchloremic acidosis.

Renal Failure

Patients with acute or chronic renal failure often develop acid-base disturbances. ABG analysis is used to:

- Assess the severity of metabolic acidosis.
- Guide the management of electrolyte imbalances.
- Monitor the effectiveness of renal replacement therapies, such as dialysis.

Critical Care and Emergency Medicine

In critical care and emergency settings, ABG analysis provides rapid and valuable information about a patient's respiratory and metabolic status.

Shock

In various forms of shock (e.g., septic, cardiogenic, hypovolemic), ABG analysis helps in:

- Assessing tissue oxygenation and perfusion.
- Detecting lactic acidosis, which indicates anaerobic metabolism.
- Guiding the management of fluid resuscitation, vasopressors, and inotropes.

Sepsis

In patients with sepsis, ABG analysis is essential for:

- Assessing the severity of metabolic acidosis and hypoxemia.
- Monitoring the response to antibiotics, fluids, and vasopressors.
- Detecting complications such as acute respiratory failure and multi-organ dysfunction.

Perioperative and Postoperative Care

ABG analysis is commonly performed in the perioperative and postoperative period to monitor respiratory and metabolic status, particularly in high-risk surgeries.

Major Surgeries

In major surgeries, especially those involving the chest or abdomen, ABG analysis helps in:

- Monitoring ventilation and oxygenation during anesthesia.
- Detecting postoperative complications such as respiratory failure and acid-base disturbances.

- Guiding the management of pain control, fluid balance, and respiratory support.

Cardiac Surgeries

In patients undergoing cardiac surgeries, ABG analysis is crucial for:

- Assessing the adequacy of oxygen delivery and carbon dioxide removal.
- Monitoring acid-base status during cardiopulmonary bypass.
- Detecting postoperative complications such as myocardial infarction and pulmonary embolism.

Chronic Illnesses

In patients with chronic illnesses, ABG analysis can provide valuable information for long-term management.

Interstitial Lung Disease (ILD)

Patients with ILD often develop progressive hypoxemia and respiratory failure. ABG analysis helps in:

- Assessing the severity of hypoxemia and hypercapnia.
- Monitoring the response to treatments such as corticosteroids and antifibrotic agents.
- Guiding the need for supplemental oxygen and ventilatory support.

Neuromuscular Disorders

In patients with neuromuscular disorders, such as amyotrophic lateral sclerosis (ALS) or muscular dystrophy, ABG analysis is used to:

- Assess respiratory muscle function and ventilation.
- Detect hypoventilation and hypercapnia, which indicate respiratory failure.
- Guide the initiation of non-invasive ventilation or mechanical ventilation.

Arterial blood gas analysis is a versatile and indispensable tool in the diagnosis and management of a wide range of conditions. Understanding the specific indications for ABG testing allows healthcare providers to utilize this tool effectively, ensuring timely and accurate assessments of respiratory and metabolic status.

MODULE FIVE

LESSON ONE: INTERPRETING ARTERIAL BLOOD GAS RESULTS

Interpreting arterial blood gas (ABG) results is a critical skill for healthcare providers. Accurate interpretation requires a systematic approach to analyze the various parameters and understand their clinical implications. This lesson will provide a step-by-step guide to ABG interpretation, helping you make informed decisions in patient care.

Step-by-Step Approach to ABG Interpretation

1. **Assess the pH**
   - The first step is to determine if the blood pH is within the normal range (7.35 to 7.45).
   - A pH below 7.35 indicates acidemia.
   - A pH above 7.45 indicates alkalemia.
2. **Evaluate PaCO2**
   - Examine the partial pressure of carbon dioxide (PaCO2) to determine if there is a respiratory component to the acid-base disturbance.
   - The normal range for PaCO2 is 35 to 45 mmHg.
   - PaCO2 below 35 mmHg suggests respiratory alkalosis (hyperventilation).
   - PaCO2 above 45 mmHg suggests respiratory acidosis (hypoventilation).
3. **Evaluate HCO3-**
   - Assess the bicarbonate (HCO3-) level to identify any metabolic component of the disturbance.
   - The normal range for HCO3- is 22 to 26 mEq/L.
   - HCO3- below 22 mEq/L indicates metabolic acidosis.

- HCO3- above 26 mEq/L indicates metabolic alkalosis.

Determine the Primary Disorder

- Compare the changes in pH, PaCO2, and HCO3- to identify the primary acid-base disorder.
- If the primary disturbance is respiratory, the pH and PaCO2 will change in opposite directions.
- If the primary disturbance is metabolic, the pH and HCO3- will change in the same direction.

Assess for Compensation

- Determine if there is compensation by the respiratory or renal systems to correct the pH imbalance.
- Respiratory compensation occurs quickly by adjusting ventilation to alter PaCO2 levels.
- Renal compensation occurs more slowly by adjusting the reabsorption or excretion of HCO3-.
- Complete compensation normalizes the pH, while partial compensation does not fully correct the pH.

Calculate the Anion Gap

- If metabolic acidosis is present, calculate the anion gap to help identify the underlying cause.
- A normal anion gap is 8 to 12 mEq/L. An elevated anion gap indicates the presence of unmeasured anions, suggesting conditions like lactic acidosis, ketoacidosis, or toxin ingestion.

COMMON ABG INTERPRETATION SCENARIOS

Respiratory Acidosis

- Causes: Hypoventilation due to COPD, drug overdose, neuromuscular disorders.
- ABG Findings:
  - ✓ pH < 7.35 (acidemia)

✓ PaCO2 > 45 mmHg (hypercapnia)

✓ HCO3- may be normal or increased if compensation is present.

Respiratory Alkalosis

- Causes: Hyperventilation due to anxiety, pain, fever, hypoxia.
- ABG Findings:
  - ✓ pH > 7.45 (alkalemia)
  - ✓ PaCO2 < 35 mmHg (hypocapnia)
  - ✓ HCO3- may be normal or decreased if compensation is present.

Metabolic Acidosis

- Causes: Diabetic ketoacidosis, renal failure, lactic acidosis, toxin ingestion.
- ABG Findings:
  - ✓ pH < 7.35 (acidemia)
  - ✓ HCO3- < 22 mEq/L (low bicarbonate)
  - ✓ PaCO2 may be normal or decreased if respiratory compensation is present.
  - ✓ Anion gap should be calculated to differentiate between anion gap and non-anion gap metabolic acidosis.

Metabolic Alkalosis

- Causes: Vomiting, diuretic use, excessive bicarbonate administration.
- ABG Findings:
  - ✓ pH > 7.45 (alkalemia)
  - ✓ HCO3- > 26 mEq/L (high bicarbonate)
  - ✓ PaCO2 may be normal or increased if respiratory compensation is present.

Mixed Acid-Base Disorders

In some cases, patients may have more than one primary acid-base disturbance simultaneously. Identifying mixed disorders involves careful analysis of pH, PaCO2, and HCO3- levels, as well as clinical context.

Examples:

- ✓ A patient with COPD and vomiting may present with both respiratory acidosis and metabolic alkalosis.
- ✓ A patient with sepsis may have lactic acidosis (metabolic acidosis) and respiratory alkalosis due to hyperventilation.

Clinical Applications

Case Study: COPD Exacerbation

- Patient: 68-year-old male with a history of COPD presents with shortness of breath.
- ABG Results:
  - ✓ pH: 7.31 (acidemia)
  - ✓ PaCO2: 58 mmHg (hypercapnia)
  - ✓ HCO3-: 28 mEq/L (compensated)
- Interpretation: The patient has respiratory acidosis with partial metabolic compensation, likely due to COPD exacerbation.

CONCLUSION

Understanding arterial blood gases (ABGs) is crucial for healthcare providers who aim to deliver high-quality care to patients with respiratory and metabolic disorders. This book has provided a comprehensive exploration of ABG analysis, from the basic physiology of blood gases to the detailed interpretation of ABG results and their clinical implications.

Arterial blood gas analysis is a powerful diagnostic tool that provides invaluable insights into a patient's physiological status. By understanding the principles and applying a systematic approach to interpretation, healthcare providers can significantly impact patient care and outcomes. As you integrate this knowledge into your practice, you will enhance your clinical acumen and contribute to the health and well-being of your patients.

This book has aimed to be both informative and engaging, providing a solid foundation in ABG analysis. As you continue your journey in healthcare, may the skills and knowledge you have gained here serve you well in your pursuit of excellence in patient care.

REFERENCES

- Arend, W. P., & Dayer, J. M. (1995). *Cytokines and cytokine inhibitors or antagonists in rheumatoid arthritis. Arthritis and Rheumatism.*

- Brubaker, R. H. (1997). *Analysis of arterial blood gases. Journal of Clinical Monitoring and Computing.*

- Carafoli, E., & Krebs, J. (2013). *Why calcium? How calcium became the best communicator. The Journal of Biological Chemistry.*

- Fanelli, A. (2001). *Pathophysiology and management of acute respiratory distress syndrome. Critical Care Medicine.*

- Ganong, W. F. (2005). *Review of Medical Physiology. McGraw-Hill Education.*

- Gennari, F. J. (2008). *Acid-base disorders and their treatment. Medical Clinics of North America.*

- Guyton, A. C., & Hall, J. E. (2006). *Textbook of Medical Physiology. Elsevier Saunders.*

- Kallen, R. J., & Ganong, W. F. (2004). *Physiology of blood gases. Journal of Clinical Chemistry.*

- Keller, G. A., & DiMagno, E. P. (1987). *Clinical and laboratory assessment of acid-base disorders. Annals of Internal Medicine.*

- Laffey, J. G., & Kavanagh, B. P. (1999). *Hypocapnia. New England Journal of Medicine.*

- Levitzky, M. G. (2003). *Pulmonary Physiology. McGraw-Hill Education.*

- Murray, J. F., & Nadel, J. A. (2000). *Textbook of Respiratory Medicine. Elsevier Health Sciences.*